Apple to Apples
Content is King, But It Isn't Everything

Stephen J. McNaughton

@SJM4K

ISBN: 1505324297
ISBN-13: 978-1505324297

INTRODUCTION

This book is part of my **VISION** series. It examines the battle for mobile supremacy between Apple's iOS and Google's Android. It explains why iOS will more than likely be the winner and how a connected world demands that successful content providers leverage these platforms to create an experience that drives consumption of the content they create. It is a must read for anyone interested in the future of technology and everyone that creates content.

It should be considered a vision of what's to come. It is intended to be broad and thought provoking. It is not intended to be an answer and should not be construed as a recommendation to purchase any of the securities referenced (or any other type of investment). Vision is preparation and my sincerest hope is that when opportunity knocks, you'll be prepared because I shared mine and helped to clarify yours.

Jonathan Swift, an Irish satirist, described **VISION** as "the art of seeing what is invisible to others". My **VISION** series is a set of papers that examine larger trends and distill them into clear, simple explanations for benefit of the curious.

CONTENTS

ACKNOWLEDGMENTS

Hursley & Betty McNaughton

1865

1

THE FUTURE OF TECH WILL BE TELEVISED

The future of tech will be televised. It will be televised to all devices with a display. The size and scope of each display will dictate the amount and type of information that's provided. Higher quality displays will receive video while lower quality displays will receive a combination of images and text. Smaller displays (or what's known as *Second Screen Technology*) will supplement larger displays to enhance the viewing experience, but all displays will be used to capture the moment instantaneously through pictures, video or commentary. More to the point, technology will allow content providers to improve the overall experience. It will enable the audience to share the experience via social media and provide related content, but more importantly free them from distraction on their main screen. The second screen will essentially become the user's gateway. It will allow them to control the experience and customize it to their own specifications. It will be the de facto remote control. It will allow viewers to consume multiple sources of content, but also more easily digest that content. For example, when watching a sporting event it could allow them to control the games' instant replay, viewing angles or keep track of another game and its' highlights. It will usurp the need for a permanent ticker at the bottom of the main viewing screen and become a more interactive way to inform the audience while keeping them tuned to events on their main viewing screen. Content consumption will be fully distributed and increasingly crowd-shared. Input from secondary devices will enable viewers to see what other viewers are saying, sharing or watching. When executed properly, content will be king and convenience will be its' queen. That's why the "utilities" of the future will not be power, water or telecommunication companies. It will be corporations that can fill or expand the space currently occupied by Google and Apple. They are the pioneers of and currently dominate this ill-formed, nascent space. Fortunately, they alone cannot own this space because the opportunity is too big; specialization will prove key.

This opportunity will be driven by sticky or better yet, Gooey Apps[i] (Gooey Applications). Google and Apple are likely to continue dominating a large share of content consumption, based on their current offerings. The companies that win, alongside Google and Apple[ii], will have to create their own Gooey Apps. These applications will exist on iOS (Apple) or Android (Google) and make it easier to digest the content that's being shared and created. A Gooey App must leverage one of these existing platforms or establish a specialized platform, that will support and sustain its' own Gooey Apps. Facebook and LinkedIn are great examples of Gooey Apps, in the making, but they didn't start as such. They are rapidly transitioning from web-based standalone portals to specialized mobile platforms that leverage iOS and Android. Facebook has particularly benefited from this transition. The majority of Facebook's user access and growth is now coming from their mobile app.

Gooey Apps will act as "Virtual Utilities" that feed the world what it craves: knowledge, entertainment, escape, connectedness, convenience, human capital, fill in the blank.... iOS is clearly the leading platform in this space, with regards to profitability. To quantify, following one of their recent product unveilings, Apple announced that they've paid over $13 billion to app developers since inception[iii]. As a platform, iOS generates significantly more for Apple than Android does for Google (per device). Horace Dediu of ASYMCO calculates[iv] based upon court documents filed in the case of *Oracle America, Inc. v. Google Inc.*[v] that Google makes roughly $1.70 per Android device. He goes on to compare this figure to Apple, who makes about $576.30 per iOS device. This figure includes income from the App Store as well as iTunes' music, movies, TV shows, iBooks, greeting cards and textbooks. More to the point, Mr. Dediu calculates that Google makes significantly more by leveraging iOS devices ($8.33) versus their own Android devices ($1.70). He concludes, *"The economics of Android are nothing like the economics of iOS."*

A Gooey App must, at minimum, leverage iOS and if it stands independently it will still need to be interoperable[vi] with iOS. Why? If the aforementioned economics haven't convinced you, please consider the following. iOS devices make up a sizeable portion of the mobile phone market; perhaps more importantly, they also have a strong position in the tablet market. While Google's Android makes up the vast majority of remaining devices, it's too fragmented to win the race against Apple without a significant strategy change. When you see a comparison between iOS and Android market share, it is often used to show that iOS is losing the race to Android; talk about burying the lede. The question of whether Apple's market share has slipped is of little relevance. The most important measure should be the profitability of its' ecosystem: user activity and content consumption. That said, many analysts continue to focus on market share as a point of comparison. So let's examine...

The mobile market is rapidly growing; the number of Android

manufacturers and their associated devices are growing with it. That means Apple is doing a yeoman's job when it comes to keeping its' market share fairly unchanged while maintaining their pricing in the face of increased competition from multiple players. It should also tell you that Apple is having a greater impact than what the purveyors of such data reflect. The part of the pie chart that reflects Android market share actually represents many companies like Acer, Amazon, LG, HTC, Kyocera and Samsung. Accordingly, comparisons between Android and iOS should not be considered Apple to Apples (pun intended).

The inherent fragmentation of the Android platform is further confused by the many versions of Android[vii] that Google allows to persist. To be fair, some of this is due to carrier restrictions. These restrictions limit the ability of customers to upgrade to newer versions of Android in the same way that they restrict device upgrades for most of their customers. All of this leaves Android developers with a lot of ground to cover and limits their ability to ensure widespread usage within the Android system. That is, if they want to sustain a solid user experience and not exhaust too much additional energy. Most developers want to focus on making their product the best it can be, NOT tailoring it over and over for endless versions of the same operating system. An even bigger challenge for these developers is keeping a consistent environment, from a security standpoint (across all the active versions of Android). The latter has restricted the speed at which this platform can be adopted by corporations and more importantly, the amount of developers willing to focus on it. Developers who decide to leverage Android often focus on the most recent versions of it for their app releases and as previously mentioned, suffer a reduction in their potential audience. In contrast, iOS users generally maintain a high adoption rate. That frees up developers to focus on the most recent version thereby maximizing their time and giving them the biggest audience for their effort.

It's already happening. Apple has been winning because they pioneered 'ease of use' and a cohesive ecosystem. They pioneered this approach when they introduced iTunes and paired it with the iPod. The pairing yielded a simple, beautiful platform that was and continues to be completely integrated. In doing so, they managed to merge their hardware and software. This merger also eliminated the compatibility issue that frustrated many Windows users when a PC from DELL, Hewlett Packard or IBM refused to interact with one another, an accessory from another company or third-party software. Apple products work together seamlessly and the resulting lack of frustration, on the part of the user, bred loyalty with a side of convenience. In this instance, convenience came in the form of a thousand songs in your pocket rather than a bag full of CDs. It also removed the need for regular trips to Tower Records or whatever music store might have been popular in your neighborhood, 10 to 15 years ago.

This was the beginning of the toll technology started to take on content. It started with the extinction of national record store chains like Tower Records and as we will discuss later, has spread to the near extinction of national movie rental locations (save localized independents). It is also currently poised to leave the same unfortunate impression on national movie theater chains. Content has become a commodity and the only thing left to differentiate content is a superior user experience with regard to how it's consumed.

2

THE MOUNTAIN TO THE MASSES

An excerpt from Chapter 12 of the Essays of Francis Bacon[viii], published in 1625, reads as follows:

"Mahomet made the people believe that he would call a hill to him, and from the top of it offer up his prayers, for the observers of his law. The people assembled; Mahomet called the hill to come to him, again and again; and when the hill stood still, he was never a whit abashed, but said, If the hill will not come to Mahomet, Mahomet will go to the hill."

In our version of the story, the hill is a mountain and the mountain is representative of content; some entities have a large piece of it while others have a small piece of it. A slightly different tack is also in order. It won't matter how much content you have, if you can't leverage it into a meaningful experience. In many instances, this will require a company to bridge the 'physical' divide of the consumer's location and the experience provided by their content. To do this, they must first bridge the 'digital' divide... A successful content provider of the future cannot rely on consumers to have the persistence of Mahomet to go to the mountain when it doesn't come. They MUST bring their piece of the mountain to the consumer. There's too much mountain to be explored and no guarantee the consumer will discover the content creator's piece of the mountain on his or her own.

Let's use Burberry, as an example. Apple recently hired its' CEO, Angela Ahrendts to run their online and retail stores. Ms. Ahrendts led a seven-year growth spurt, at Burberry, by bridging the 'digital' divide. She focused the company on integrating Apple's iPad in their stores and used the iPhone to film its' fashion shows[ix]. Her goal was to enhance the experience of Burberry's customers by leveraging Apple's iOS platform. In a 2010 article by *The Wall Street Journal*, she was quoted as saying she didn't compare Burberry's strategy with peers such as Gucci and Chanel… "If I look to any company as a model, it's Apple," she said. "They're a brilliant design company working to create a lifestyle, and that's the way I see us." In other words, she doesn't compare Burberry, a fashion company, to other fashion companies. She was focused on emulating a company that pioneered creating an experience for its' consumers and making products that were an extension of that experience. In doing so, she enhanced and leveraged their brand in a way that allowed their customer base to participate in Burberry's experience. Customers weren't just buying products, they were participating in an experience and when they bought the company's clothing they were able to own that experience. More to the point, by leveraging technology it was an experience Burberry made them want. The approach worked and as a result of Ms. Ahrendt's leadership, the company's stock increased 200% while revenues doubled. Ms. Ahrendt's experience, at what was considered a fading 150 year-old fashion house, shows that if the masses can't or won't come to the mountain; a connected world demands that the mountain be brought to them. The future success of many entities will depend on it. Content comes in many shapes and sizes; be it clothing, video, print, music or the tools used to create and share the aforementioned, but technology will be an inseparable part of all content going forward.

3

THE FUTURE OF TECH IS BEING TELEGRAPHED

The future of tech and content is being telegraphed. The trick to successfully getting your audience to consume your content will be in the delivery, the experience. Let's continue with the example of digital music… Ironically, as any audiophile will tell you, the quality of an MP3 is poor when compared to other storage formats. CDs have an edge when it comes to quality, but they aren't a convenient way to take the show on the road. If you love music, why would you replace a CD with an MP3?

It seems obvious, right? Consumers are willing to sacrifice quality for convenience and that's the lesson that many tech and media companies learned from the success of the portable MP3 player. CORRECTION: That's what less than innovative companies learned. More innovative companies also realized that consumers are only willing to sacrifice quality, if they are given a superior experience. The experience had to translate beyond being able to take lots of music with you. It didn't just have to be easy to take music with you; it also had to be easy to get music, sort it, build playlists and ultimately, listen to it. That's why initial stabs at the portable music industry from stalwarts like Sony, who created *The*

Walkman (the original portable music player), had only been successful in creating a fragmented array of portable digital music players. Not surprisingly, very little progress was made toward making the MP3 the de facto standard for music consumption during that period. Apple did not invent the MP3 or even the portable digital music player, but by pairing the iPod with iTunes they created an experience. An experience that allowed the user to manage their existing library, acquire additional songs that they heard on the radio and update their device in the most streamlined way, to that point. Don't get us wrong.... iTunes was by no means perfect at release, but it got over the hurdle enough to make a little bit of frustration worth the pleasure of leaving the house with most of your music library in hand.

Once they got the formula, Apple kept tweaking it until they were the dominant platform for listening (iPod) to music and distributing (iTunes) it. Apple didn't destroy the music industry; it prolonged the inevitable. On a long enough timeline, the growth rate for every industry, and the companies that compose it, drops to zero. The companies that buck this trend never stop asking questions: How do we change our business model, enter new markets and become more efficient so that we don't become a casualty of the progress we seek to embody? The music industry is not dead, but it needs to create a new experience and update its' business model. In a connected world with plenty of content, the industry is another commodity. That's not to say there won't be standouts like Lady Gaga and U2, who can charge a premium and are somewhat recession proof, but that won't last forever. The very few that can maintain demand, even in death, can be counted on one hand e.g. Michael Jackson and Elvis Presley. The future will require an experience and the questions the music industry should start asking are... Why have the bulk of our performers historically made most of their money on tour? Why are we really not able to sell more albums in a digital world? If you think the answer is piracy or the MP3, you'd be wrong. In a connected world, if you want people to buy your content it has to be about the experience.

How do you bring the concert experience to the devices of the masses in a way that holds their attention and makes them want to buy a song because it reminds them of that experience? This is not about having a Twitter feed. Nor is it about getting attendees to tweet about an event to people who aren't at said event and could probably care less. It's about bringing that experience home to the many that only go to a few concerts a year or perhaps, have never been to a concert.

In a connected world you have to bring your piece of the mountain to them and make them buy a song to remember the experience or tempt them to go to your piece of the mountain themselves. The first company to truly crack the code on how to do this will win the day and revolutionize the music industry. Remember, content is and always will be king, but it will never again tax the people without giving them their money's worth. In other words, content owners won't make premium dollars for content until they can leverage content into a premium experience. In doing so, they'll succeed in delaying their descent to zero and create a more profitable future.

The dream of this profitable future is why Microsoft acquired Nokia and Google acquired Motorola. They are attempting to replicate Apple's integrated experience. This experience was in question when Microsoft dominated a PC centered world, but its' relevance has been proven as the world has transformed to a more mobile experience. You can't have convenience without ease of use and a great experience. To create such an experience, it requires a level of control and an eye for the details. That's why Apple has been successful. They've been able to expand the experience of their software to their hardware thereby creating an experience that feels complete. They have been able to capitalize on this opportunity as a direct result of their late, co-founder Steve Jobs' vision. This vision was crystallized when he famously proclaimed that we are in the "Post PC" era.

To capture the Apple magic, Microsoft and Google will need more than control of their hardware and the requisite integration. They'll need to create a vision that taps into the experience of their brand, translates into an experience that resonates with their users and makes those users want to own that experience. Apple has a cool factor and is widely considered to be a high-end brand. It will be difficult for Google or Microsoft to capture this space, but not impossible. They are better off carving out their own experience. They can define themselves as the brand for the technologically savvy or even a visionary of a better experience, but it must be derived from their corporate culture. Why can't Google or Microsoft become the cool or premium brand? The answer is simple. It's very difficult to supplant an incumbent once they've been defined in the minds of the public as representative of a specific quality.

For more detail on this phenomenon, please research the soda wars. Coke was the incumbent and considered to be synonymous with soda. Pepsi tried for many years to supplant Coke, but was unable to mount a real challenge until they went after new categories in the market place. This trend is very clear. The need to create new categories like diet, caffeine-free and sports drinks to grab market share can be seen in many product categories, but we'll save that discussion for a future white paper.

The same questions or, perhaps more appropriately, reality has begun to rear its head in the television and movie industries. They may choose to ignore them, but it will be at their own peril. Truthfully, they are in a worse position than the recording industry. The best movies or classics of the past are already in the $5 bin at Wal-Mart. If a newer movie hasn't made it to the bin yet, you may be able to see it On-Demand via an existing subscription to Netflix or Amazon Prime. Worse yet, for the creators of such content, if you've got a little patience you'll probably see an edited version randomly broadcast on television or the uncut original on HBO, Showtime or Starz. The movie and television industries have been content to delay the inevitability of a life in reruns by delaying the period between a limited release at theaters and when you can buy it to watch, as many times as you want, from the privacy of your home. To survive the fate of the recording industry, they must learn that it's NOT about being content; it's about having content and the experience it creates for the consumer.

Movie theaters are winning the race to zero, for many reasons. They are facing a serious problem. Technology is getting so good that the price to watch a movie at the theater, drive, park and grab snacks isn't quite low enough to offset the value or convenience of kicking up your feet in the living room with your big screen, high definition video and surround sound system from the comfort of your armchair. The only thing sustaining this part of the movie industry is the willingness of the studios to indulge the worst qualities of theater chains and comfort with the status quo. It's easier to preserve short-term profits than adapt to what's coming and ensure a sustainable long-term path. There will always be a few people that head to the movies, but unfortunately they won't be enough to sustain the industry without a strategy change. Home theater technology is getting too good and the price to acquire and install it is getting to be cheap. Movie theaters like AMC and Regal must adapt by creating an experience that expands beyond the timing of releases. They can't rely on the fact that studio blockbusters are currently released to them first. As it stands, their status as first stop in the distribution process is their last advantage.

How long could theaters sustain themselves if content owners (studios) realize they can make more money by going directly to consumers? They are already doing it in limited ways, by allowing consumers to watch movies that are currently in theaters via services like LodgeNet (in hotels), for a premium price. Worse yet, independent films are expanding this option via services like Video On Demand (from the likes of Comcast and DirecTV) or Digital Distribution via Amazon Prime and Netflix. This trend highlights that theaters are becoming a less essential part of the distribution channel. To survive, they have to create an experience that drives demand. They must become indispensable, as an avenue of distribution, for the movie industry by creating an experience that allows them to charge a premium. This will mean a higher return for studios and prompt individuals not to wait for new movie content to become available via Netflix or Amazon Prime due to convenience. The more movie theaters can become an alternate distribution channel, the more they can counter the downward pressure on the pricing of content provided by studios to increase their requisite market share and stave off Amazon and Netflix.

Conversely, the digital distribution channels (currently represented by Amazon and Netflix) know that they are currently dependent on the movie industry (studios) for content. They are steadily shoring up their own positions so they can truly add downward pressure to the pricing of these content providers by not being dependent on them, indefinitely. The reality of this race to zero was the impetus for Comcast (another distribution channel) to buy NBC Universal. It is why Netflix and Amazon are starting to create their own original content. It gives them a way to lure more consumers, but more importantly allows them the leverage needed to negotiate with content providers and ultimately, lower their future rates to add third party content. If they don't need to acquire outside content and third party providers don't have their own distribution channels, they will have leverage when it comes to negotiating costs. In the short term, Amazon and Netflix are following the HBO blueprint. Unfortunately for Amazon, Comcast, Netflix and even HBO itself... HBO's blueprint is unfinished. HBOs success started when it began creating original content, like *The Sopranos* and *The Wire*. This content drove consumers to purchase subscriptions for HBO because they wanted high quality, commercial-free content and the experience provided by these shows. These shows literally put HBO on the map and that's evidenced by the contract they awarded to the late, James Gandolfini. Following a contract dispute, regarding how much he would be paid to continue appearing as the lead character of *The Sopranos* he was awarded $13 million. It should be noted, at the time of the contract, HBO was generally considered to be valued at $100 million. More to the point, although original programming like *The Sopranos* helped establish HBO, as a premier brand, it still didn't connect the brand to its' users in a meaningful enough way. This was recently underscored by virtue of Netflix exceeding HBO in paid subscribers during October of 2013. For context, consider that HBO has been around since 1972 and Netflix was founded in 1997.

Additionally, it put HBO in the unenviable position of having to continue creating new shows to replace its' early successes and retain its' audience. Let's call these successes, mini-experiences that are needed to encourage viewers to purchase and maintain subscriptions to HBO's content. To this day, many viewers drop their subscription and then re-establish it when they know new episodes of their favorite shows are due to air. It's clear that to win, content will not be enough... Each of these entities, whether it's Comcast, HBO, Amazon or Netflix will need to create a truly great experience for the consumer that exceeds accessibility and quality of content. They must allow their viewers to own the experience of their brand, in a way that resonates. Fortunately for HBO, the other companies referenced have a similar challenge and we are only in the early stages of this transition. Although Amazon and Netflix seem to be leading the way because they are able to connect through technology and accessibility, if they aren't careful they may fall to Apple's more complete blueprint or one developed by another competitor.

Apple has shaped an experience which Ms. Ahrendt's keyed into at Burberry because she recognized that Apple was a lifestyle for its' users. It had a coolness that was reflected in its' form factor and translated to the lifestyle of its' users. That's why many content providers currently have streaming apps that leverage iOS. The Comcasts and HBOs of the world need to create their own experience that translates into a lifestyle or at least, an emotion for their users. They don't have to do it themselves. They can continue to leverage the Apple experience, like Ms. Ahrendt's did at Burberry, to enhance their brands or become more of a specialized platform and develop a niche that's specific to the majority of their users. To do so, they will have to make their current apps more than the placeholders that they are currently. In the next five years, it will be imperative that all of these entities finish their blueprint. If they plan to survive and connect to their user base, in a meaningful way, they must become more than distribution channels.

There's a pattern emerging. It began with print media (which isn't discussed in this report), spread to audio and is nearly ready to infect video. Technology is reducing the cost of producing content, but also restricting the price that can be charged to acquire such content. These industries have a chance to capitalize on technology and own their destiny. Their path to profitability and the amount of near term pain experienced will depend on their willingness to accept that things are changing. They must create a complete blueprint that engages the consumers of their content. The television and movie industries have the opportunity to avoid the missteps of the print and music industries, but they can't be lulled to sleep by a serenade of technologies that have given their industries the false hope of past technological evolutions. These evolutions e.g. the DVD, Blu-Ray and internet, which yielded high quality streaming, have postponed the inevitable loss in pricing power that plagues all industries when their products become a commodity. The only exceptions to this rule are industries where the commodity is limited in supply e.g. energy, food, etc.

In the back of their collective minds, the movie industry knows this and they've manipulated things like the window between theatrical release and home viewing over the years to maintain premium pricing. They've also used it to encourage the adoption of storage formats like Blu-Ray, which they believed would support and sustain better pricing. When the availability of home videos became popular, as a result of the broad acceptance of VHS, the average time between theatrical release and the distribution for home rental was roughly one year. The ability to purchase a VHS copy, for home ownership, was even further down the road. This was intended to support the distribution channel represented by rental companies like Blockbuster and Hollywood Video. The release of higher quality viewing options like the DVD and Blu-Ray has further reduced the release period to somewhere between three and four months. Netflix helped to destroy this model when it started delivering movies for home viewing, digitally. The result was the virtual extinction of the physical rental store, despite the movie industry's attempts to sustain it. Coincidentally, the gap between home rental and home ownership has also virtually disappeared in the digital age. The most immediate reason was pricing. Netflix priced their offerings, at a level that was commensurate to their true cost of content acquisition and delivery. Combined with their lack of a physical footprint and the convenience of digital distribution, they've been able to grab significant market share. If they can continue lowering their acquisition costs for content, when paired with the variety of their offerings, they will be able to increase their profitability.

Netflix is extremely close to a sustainable model, but they are still lacking when it comes to creating an experience for their audience. The latter is best evidenced by their failed 2011 Qwikster[x] experiment. This experiment was intended to separate their DVD by mail business from their streaming business (which would have retained the Netflix name). They hoped that this would allow them to raise prices by charging a premium to individuals, who wanted to stream videos and retain the option to order DVDs by mail. This decision was made in the best interest of Netflix and its' profitability. It's difficult to create a great customer experience when the thought process for that experience doesn't begin with the customer. Despite this hiccup, Netflix is generally on the right track because they are testing new models for content delivery and that is what success in the future of content distribution will require. Traditional movie rental companies missed their window and are on the verge of extinction because they refused to rethink their business model.

The following graph is a great illustration of the impact Netflix and newer distribution formats are having on the movie industry:

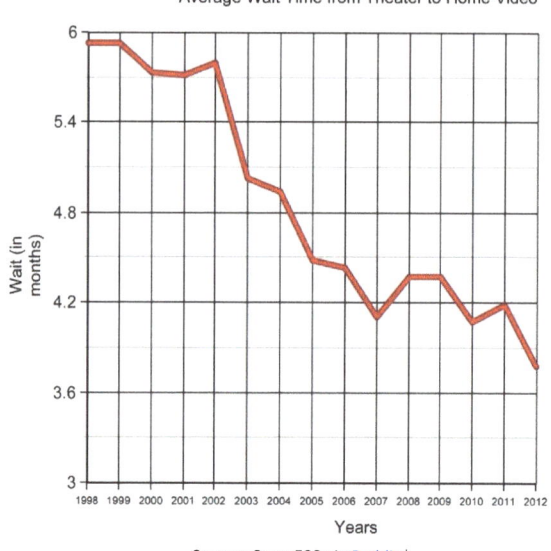

Average Wait Time from Theater to Home Video

Source: Steve599 via Reddit[xi]

As context for this graph, we've compiled a brief timeline for the release of these newer formats below:

Broad Acceptance	Format
1977	VHS
1997	DVD
2006	Blu-Ray
2008	On-Demand Video
2010	Streaming Video

Despite significant damage to the first two legs (theater and rental) of the movie industry's distribution channels, they seem intent to also let their last leg (home ownership) die on the vine. The current price to download a digital, high-definition (HD) copy of a movie is unsustainable. Yes, it's cheaper than Blu-Ray, but at $19.99 it's still too expensive! No shipping, no packaging and yet, it costs the same amount we used to pay to buy a movie when DVDs first became available for public consumption. Let's do a current comparison of some other forms of content in similar formats... HD versions of some of the most popular television shows (40 minutes running time) are currently available on Amazon Prime for $1.29 per episode if you buy the season or $1.99 if you purchase, per episode. In contrast, a HD full-length movie with running time of an hour and a half is available for $19.99. Amazon sells the standard definition version for $14.99[1]. In contrast, the Blu-Ray version with a standard DVD and digital copy is available for $29.99. The latter package pricing for Blu-Ray shows that studios understand more attractive pricing, from their standpoint, requires more content. Unfortunately, they still don't get that content isn't enough... The longevity of this pricing will require a better experience. People are willing to pay this pricing in the short-term because they want to own it first, but this type of thinking is a short-term, quantitative decision (NOT a value additive one). It only takes one; the first studio to connect with the audience and reduce its' prices to a level commensurate with their lower cost of production and distribution, will take significant market share. If they can also supplement that pricing with a better experience, they will be able to assign premium pricing to certain offerings and profitability will follow. Content is widely available, but a great experience is not.

Unlike the profit model for home video ownership, the profit model

---

[1] FYI: Since the initial release of this white paper, we've already started to see some studios like Universal Pictures start to experiment with the pricing of their digital offerings. $14.99 is now the price for some of their new HD offerings and the standard definition version now retails for a slightly more reasonable, $12.99.

for rentals has already changed; it changed along with its' primary delivery format because Netflix forced that change. Many people blame Netflix for the reduced profitability of rentals in the same way that Apple is blamed for the downfall of the music industry's profitability. The truth is that the movie industry like the music industry has refused to add value and lacked creativity when it comes to their business model. The studios are positioned, after losing two profit centers due to the lack of a credible approach, to forfeit their last profit center (home ownership) in the same way. If they don't create this change by thinking differently, it will be done for them; an outside player (like Netflix or maybe even Netflix itself) will change it for them. If that happens, movie studios may lose their ability to dictate the way films are distributed in the future. Inherent in that loss of control, will be a total loss of pricing power. Unfortunately for movie theaters, the studios will survive. The studios will be less profitable, but they will survive and movie theaters will end up sharing the fate of Blockbuster and Hollywood Video.

4

THE FUTURE OF TECH WILL BE INTERACTIVE, COMMUNAL AND ABOUT THE MOMENT

Content will need to become more interactive to translate to an experience that captivates and brings the mountain to the masses. A natural next step seems like it should involve live television in the form of concerts or sports. It must give users access to parts of the event in ways they might not get, even if they were at the event venue. It must connect viewers to the event and equally important, viewers to each other. In the world of sport, it could mean giving viewers access to pre-game speeches, bringing them into the huddle, onto the sidelines and making them part of post-game interviews. Content creators must give consumers more of what they want.

Flashes of this interaction can currently be seen, in a limited way, at the movies.... Despite the almost too prevalent amount of advertising, people still show up early for a movie to see the pre-game (movie trailers). Theaters have a captive audience, in that moment, and know exactly what they want. The audience loves it because they are there to see a movie and they are being given more of what they came to see as well as a glimpse into what future movie experiences might hold. To encourage audiences to consume more content, advertising and content have to become locationally aware. They must be aware of the audience, but also time and place with respect to the audience. Content providers must bring the mountain to consumers when and where they want it, not when and where the content providers want it. If it's done on the consumer's terms, they will be receptive and more likely to retain the experience. Success will require companies that win the future, represented by the content hungry public, to drive consumption by blending technology, content and communication in a way that creates the best experience for the consumer. This will be measured by their ability to leverage their brand into a lifestyle that resonates with their consumers. They must make consumers want to own the experience of their brand.

I'll save the specifics of how this might be achieved for a future white paper... I hope you've found my commentary to be thought provoking. I've covered a lot of ground and have a lot more ground to cover. I'm also hopeful that I clearly articulated the need for content creators / providers to rethink their business models, push harder to create a better, more cohesive experience and their inherent opportunity for redemption.

5

DISCLAIMERS

This white paper represents the opinions of Stephen J. McNaughton. The information contained in this white paper is based on publicly available information with respect to the industries and companies mentioned, as of the date it was published. Mr. McNaughton has not sought or obtained consent from any third party to use any statements or information, which are described in this white paper that have been obtained or derived from statements made or published by third parties. Any such statements or information should not be viewed as indicating the support of such third party for the views expressed in this white paper. No warranty is made that data or information, whether derived or obtained from filings made with the Securities and Exchange Commission or any other regulatory agency or from any third party, are accurate. This white paper is not intended to be, nor should it be construed as, an offer to sell or a solicitation of an offer to buy any security. This white paper does not recommend the purchase or sale of any security.

Any illustrations presented are done solely for educational and informational purposes; they are not intended for trading purposes, or intended to be considered as investment advice. Any performance results, reference to performance results and / or illustration of performance results related to the companies and / or sectors discussed exclude the effects of taxes, brokerage commissions and any other expenses that are typically incurred when investing. No representation is made that this document or any other commentary on the part of Stephen J. McNaughton should be perceived as investment advice. Additionally, the historical performance of the companies and / or sectors referenced should not be used to infer any benefit with regard to the application of any of the ideas shared to a particular investment strategy. Should you choose, on your own, to apply the ideas presented in these materials, it should not be construed as validation of a successful investment strategy or a recommendation by Stephen J. McNaughton.

The opinions expressed are subject to change without notice and do not take into account the particular investment objectives, financial situation or needs of individual investors. Leviathan Capital ® does not sponsor, endorse, sell, promote or manage any investment fund or other investment vehicle that is offered by third parties. A decision to invest in any investment vehicle should not be made in reliance on any of the statements set forth in this document.

Past performance of the securities and / or sectors discussed is not and should not be viewed as indicative of future performance. Should you choose to make investment decisions after reading this document, they should be considered entirely your own and are made at your own risk.

Additional Information: May Be Available Upon Request.

Leviathan Capital IP ® is a subsidiary of Leviathan Capital, LLC ® ("GP"). It owns and maintains all of the intellectual property that's created by Stephen J. McNaughton. Its intellectual property includes, but is not limited to this document as well as many other copyrights, trademarks and patents.

For the latest TECH news, please follow me: **@SJM4K**

www.SJM4K.com

ABOUT THE AUTHOR

Stephen J. McNaughton

Chaucer once said, *"Time and tide wait for no man"*. This quote is often paraphrased as *"Life waits for no one"*. While both quotes are true in the strictest sense, they fail to define time and life. First, time is often clumsily interpreted as life. Time begins at birth. It's always moving forward regardless of whether we engage it. Second, life requires engagement and begins when we decide to start living it. I prefer Churchill's perspective...

In his words, *"To improve is to change... To be perfect is to change often"*. If a quote could sum up the entirety of one's life, this would capture mine. A constant pursuit to find challenges that improve & expand the talents I've been blessed with; an artist at heart, advisor by profession and the author of my destiny. I seek constant, and in some cases incremental, change. I'm tireless in my focus on improvement and approach each challenge according to my core values: PATIENCE, PERSISTENCE and DISCIPLINE. Challenges are necessary because overcoming them breeds confidence and ultimately success, no matter how small. With each challenge conquered, I find myself improved for taking the challenge. Perfection is not within the grasp of man, but seeking it allows for constant improvement and fulfillment. The pursuit is filled with failure and success, but it makes life worth living. I choose life and everything that's waiting.

I am currently the CEO of Rede Wealth ®, an independent wealth management firm, and have been in the wealth management industry for 15 years. After graduating from the University of Virginia, I began my career as a Wealth Advisor at one of the largest global wealth management firms in the world. During my time there, I became the youngest Branch Manager in the firm, at the age of 26. I am passionate about helping clients meet their financial goals by empowering them to take control of their financial world and create their own *Investment Process and Philosophy*.

CHALLENGES WANTED. MOUNTAIN PEAKS. LIFE WAITS. ™

REFERENCES

---

[i] I named this space after the two companies who are pioneering it: Google & Apple.

[ii] I have specifically chosen not to directly discuss Samsung in this article because while they have a significant portion of the market for phones / tablets, they do not control a large part of their user experience in the form of software. They are dependent on Google for the Android operating system and as a result do not have a truly integrated experience. This will make it difficult for them to have long-term success and has already resulted in a fragmented developer experience with limited application development. It has also created potential security issues and resulted in a limited user experience. Samsung is dependent on Google's charity and they risk mass user defection if Google decides to be less charitable with their software updates or even make Android more proprietary for their own use when distributing the hardware manufactured by their new hardware unit, Motorola. There are some Samsung fans that might deny the idea of Google ceasing to support Android for broad use, but the reality is that Google makes very little revenue from the distribution of Android for use by third parties. More to the point, should Google choose the latter, it's likely that many Samsung users would defect to a proprietary Google product or worse yet, Apple. The integration of hardware and software will be essential to an integrated, cohesive experience. The risk posed by Samsung's dependence on another company for its' operating system is too great to ignore and leaves a greater risk with respect to their ability to create an integrated experience that can win the future of content consumption.

iii http://techcrunch.com/2013/10/22/1-million-apps-later-apple-says-developers-have-made-13-billion-on-its-platform/

iv http://www.asymco.com/2012/04/02/android-economics/

v http://cand.uscourts.gov/wha/oraclevgoogle/docs

vi At this point, iOS doesn't allow outside apps to be interoperable unless they build an exclusive app for iOS, but we believe this will change as Apple begins to more fully realize the potential of its' platform. Right now, Apple limits this interoperability to preferred providers, like Yahoo, to feed information to their proprietary apps like weather and stocks. It is not a leap to think they will open such channels to additional access from other third-party developers. This doesn't mean they will cede control of their ecosystem. They will certainly maintain the high level of quality control that they've become known for while setting clear standards for third-party access that enhances the consumer's experience.

vii http://en.wikipedia.org/wiki/Android_version_history

viii Francis Bacon, Essays, Chapter 12

ix http://www.apple.com/pr/library/2013/09/12Burberry-Uses-iPhone-5s-to-Capture-Spring-Summer-2014-Runway- Show.html

x http://online.wsj.com/news/articles/SB10001424052970203499704576622674082410578

xihttp://www.reddit.com/r/movies/comments/z1393/for_the_past_couple_days_i_have_been_researching/

THIS BOOK IS NOT INTENDED TO BE, NOR SHOULD IT BE CONSTRUED AS AN OFFER TO SELL OR A SOLICITATION OF AN OFFER TO BUY ANY SECURITY. THIS WHITE PAPER DOES NOT RECOMMEND THE PURCHASE OR SALE OF ANY SECURITY.

www.ingramcontent.com/pod-product-compliance
Lightning Source LLC
Chambersburg PA
CBHW040819200526
45159CB00024B/3040